CRAZY but PIECEABLE

Eight Charming Patterns to Make and Enjoy

Enjoy
Hollie Milne

Hollie A. Milne

*"I'm glad I never threw them away;
my scraps of yore are my quilts today."*
Sandra L. O'Brien
Great American Quilts
1988

Acknowledgments

Many thanks to:

My husband, Gordon, for the support and love which have enabled me to pursue my dream; my daughter Merideth, for designing the angel and watering cans; my daughter Allison, for tracing the crazy patchwork patterns; my daughter Joy, for removing the freezer paper and appliqué film from the pattern pieces; and my sons, Bradley and David, for giving me pats on the back—I love you all.

The Ruby Tuesday Ladies, for being my friends and for encouraging me to write this book: Barbara Gibson, for proofreading the instructions and making "Home on the Range"; Valerie Harker, for writing my biography; Ruth Walburger, for making "Twinkle, Twinkle"; and Toni Young, for testing some of the patterns.

That Patchwork Place, for making my dream a reality.

Dedication

This book is dedicated to my cheerleaders: Gordon, Bradley, David, Merideth, Allison, and Joy.

Mission Statement

We are dedicated to providing quality products and service by working together to inspire creativity and to enrich the lives we touch.

Cover quilt:

Spring Harvest

by Hollie Milne, 1996,
Calgary, Alberta, Canada, 26" x 26".

Credits

Editor-in-Chief . . . . Kerry I. Smith
Technical Editor . . . . Melissa A. Lowe
Managing Editor . . . . .Judy Petry
Design Director . . . . Cheryl Stevenson
Text and Cover Designer . . . . Kay Green
Production Assistant . . . . Claudia L'Heureux
Copy Editor . . . . Liz McGehee
Proofreader . . . . Leslie Phillips
Illustrator . . . . Laurel Strand
Decorative Art . . . . Barb Tourtillotte
Photographer . . . . Brent Kane

Crazy but Pieceable:
Eight Charming Patterns to Make and Enjoy
©1997 by Hollie A. Milne

That Patchwork Place, Inc.,
PO Box 118,
Bothell, WA 98041-0118 USA

Printed in the United States of America
02 01 00 99 98 97   6 5 4 3 2 1

Library of Congress Cataloging-in-Publication Data

Milne, Hollie A.,
     Crazy but pieceable : eight charming patterns to make and enjoy / Hollie A. Milne.
          p.   cm.
     ISBN 1-56477-190-3
     1. Patchwork—Patterns. 2. Quilting—Patterns.
     3. Crazy quilts. I. Title
TT385.M45 1997
746.46'041—dc21   97-9752
                                                              CIP

Contents

Introduction

Quilting is a unique form of art—it warms us, soothes us, and connects us with our past. I quilt for the emotional as well as the physical warmth my quilts give me, my family, and my friends. I began quilting when I was in college because I was *cold*. As I grew older, my quilting developed around my family—changing focus and growing as my family grew. I cross-stitched and hand quilted a quilt for my first baby, pieced a quilt for my second baby, began giving quilts to family and friends after my third baby, began teaching after my fourth baby, and began designing quilts and machine quilting after my fifth baby.

I've made more than one hundred quilts since I began quilting, and my students often ask, "Which is your favorite?" My favorite quilt is always the one I'm working on—especially if it has crazy patchwork. This book is my opportunity to share my techniques and timesaving tips for making crazy-patch quilts. There are eight easy projects you can make, using freezer-paper piecing and fusible appliqué, creative variations for each pattern, and ideas for creating your own crazy patchwork designs.

Whether you are a beginning or an expert quilter, I hope you have as much fun making the projects in this book as I have. Above all, enjoy the process as you explore the world of crazy patchwork.

Getting Started

Crazy but Pieceable is for everyone who loves crazy patchwork, but doesn't want to go crazy trying to make a crazy patchwork quilt. In the traditional method for crazy patchwork quilting, you laboriously piece odd shapes of fabric on muslin or paper foundations. This is a frustrating process because, more often than not, you end up without enough fabric to cover the foundation.

Using the method in this book, you can create easy crazy patchwork with freezer-paper piecing, your rotary cutter, and a sewing machine. All of the projects are made with crazy patchwork blocks, used either as backgrounds for appliqué or in the borders.

To help you get started, I have included some invaluable tricks of the trade. See "Fabric: The Quilter's Palette" (pages 5–6). This section explains how to select and use fabric to set the mood of your quilt as well as how to prepare your fabric for quiltmaking. "The Quilter's Sewing Basket" (pages 7–8) describes the supplies and tools you will need to make the projects. "The Quilter's Beginning Basics" (page 9) provides basic quiltmaking instructions and tips. For step-by-step instructions, look at "The Construction Techniques" (pages 10–13) and "The Projects" (pages 13–49). "The Finishing Touches" (pages 50–55) includes assembling and finishing basics as well as special touches you can use to make your quilts unique. Finally, "Signing Your Quilt" (page 55) has ideas for labeling your quilt. A quilt is not complete until it is signed and dated! (Be sure to look through the projects for other label ideas.) The crazy patchwork patterns and appliqué templates are provided on the pullout.

Fabric: The Quilter's Palette

You are an artist, your quilt is your artwork, and fabric is your palette. The style, print, and color of the fabric you choose all help communicate a mood. For example, some fabrics seem romantic, while others seem fun or whimsical. Be sure you select fabrics that communicate the mood and theme you want. For ideas, look at "For the Birds and the Bees" and "Everything Grows Better with Love" (page 25). "For the Birds and the Bees" feels whimsical, but the creative interpretation feels romantic.

When it's time to choose colors, step out of your comfort zone. Trust your instincts and be courageous. Choose colors that you wouldn't normally use. If you choose beige as the predominant color, as in "Legacy" (page 30), add a bit of white. The white handkerchief decorating the basket adds sparkle. Finally, try adding a "zinger." Look at "Nurture Friendships" (page 29); the red Yo-yos and binding give the quilt contrast and zing.

If you look at "'Tis the Season" and "Around the Christmas Table" (page 32), you'll notice that I like using plaids as part of my fabric palette, and I don't worry about keeping the plaid straight when cutting. That's part of the charm of crazy patchwork: it isn't supposed to be perfect.

 TIP

One of the tricks of quiltmaking is that adding what you think of as an "ugly" color can make your quilt sing. Look at the fabrics languishing in your fabric stash; you might find the perfect accent. (If you are a new quilter, a fabric "stash" is a collection of fabrics bought for some future quilt or project. Quilters have been known to stash their fabrics around the house and in the trunks of their cars so their families won't know just how much they have.)

WHAT FABRICS SHOULD I CHOOSE?

Begin with high-quality, 100% cotton fabric. Not only are these fabrics easier to work with, they hold up better over time. If you want your crazy patchwork quilt to be interesting, you need both variety and contrast: a variety of fabrics for the crazy patchwork, and contrast between the background and appliqué fabrics. This is just as important in a two-color quilt like "Look Up at the Stars" (page 27) as it is in a multicolored quilt like "For the Birds and the Bees" (page 25).

When choosing fabrics for the crazy patchwork, think about where it will be. If you are using the crazy patchwork as a background, choose one color and value (the lightness or darkness of the color). If you are using crazy patchwork in the border, choose many fabrics in different colors and values. For an example, look at "Love Notes" (page 30).

How many fabrics should you choose for the crazy patchwork? My rule of thumb: whatever size crazy patchwork square I am making, I use that many fabrics. For example, for a 10" square, I use ten fabrics. Use many different patterns and designs to add interest.

Contrast is especially important for appliqué. Look at the appliqué fabrics used in "Nesting Instinct" (page 31). If the appliqué fabrics do not contrast with the background fabrics, you won't be able to distinguish the design. I recommend "auditioning" different fabrics for the appliqué pieces. Choose several fabrics you like, then compare them with the background to determine which fabric looks best.

 TIP

Follow this easy fabric recipe for creating crazy patchwork.
- Choose one fabric in a color or colors you like.
- Add several related fabrics from your fabric stash. (If you do not have a fabric stash, look for fat-quarter packets at your local quilt shop.)
- Mix in some new fabrics that coordinate with the old.
- Choose appliqué fabrics that complement the crazy patchwork. (Remember to choose colors and values that also contrast with the crazy patchwork if you are using it as a background.)

HOW MUCH FABRIC IS ENOUGH?

The measurements in this book are based on 44"-wide fabric, but you'll find that I always give you a little extra. This should cover shrinkage, if you prewash, and little mistakes. (Even the most experienced quilter can make a mistake.) If you have been "stashing" fabric for a long time, you will probably only need a few new fabrics. Buy the smallest amount your quilt shop will sell you, or try precut fat quarters.

I like to increase my fabric stash as my budget permits. Do try to keep up with fabric trends. If a color (like yellow) is usually hard to find, try to buy it when you see it. Another way to increase your stash is by swapping with friends. Remember, a quilter can *never* have enough fabric.

SHOULD I PREWASH OR NOT?

As a teacher, I hear this question a lot. I admit it: I don't prewash my fabrics. I have several good reasons for not prewashing:
- I like the crisp feel of new fabric.
- I hate ironing fabric after I wash it.
- High-quality fabrics are usually colorfast and shrink a minimal amount.
- Above all, I am usually too eager to use the fabric.

I think prewashing can give a false sense of security. Prewashing does not stop a fabric from running or bleeding; the fabric dye may still bleed if you wash the finished quilt, especially if you didn't use high-quality fabric. If you are concerned about bleeding, place a small piece of the fabric in a jar with warm water and a small amount of detergent. Shake the jar. If the fabric bleeds (the water changes color), you need to set the dye. Prewash the fabric in your washing machine, adding two cups of white vinegar to the rinse cycle. Repeat the test. If the fabric still bleeds, do not use it in your quilt.

 TIP

Before buying fabric, rub your fingers over it. If the fabric dye rubs off on your fingers, do not buy it. Always test deep red and purple fabrics before using them in your quilts. These colors are prone to bleeding.

The Quilter's Sewing Basket

In addition to fabric, you will need the following basic quiltmaking supplies and tools. Remember, the proper tools make any job easier and faster.

 **TIP**

Having a work space you can call your own will make your quiltmaking much more pleasant. Find a space in your home where you can work without having to put everything away every time you find a few minutes to sew. You need space for rotary cutting, sewing, and pressing. If possible, include an area for a design wall and for storing quiltmaking supplies and tools, such as fabric, thread, rotary cutters, acrylic rulers, books, and patterns.

SUPPLIES

Tissue Paper

I use the white tissue paper designed for gift wrapping. To start your project, trace a crazy patchwork pattern onto the tissue paper. Use this as a master pattern.

Freezer Paper

The shiny side of freezer paper has a light coating of wax. When pressed onto fabric, the wax adheres the freezer paper to the fabric. Freezer paper does not leave a residue when it is removed.

When you make these projects, you trace a crazy patchwork pattern onto freezer paper, cut it apart, then iron the freezer-paper templates onto your fabrics. The templates help prevent bias edges from stretching and provide straight edges for sewing.

Fusible Web

The appliqué pieces in these projects are attached with fusible web. A light- or medium-weight fusible web gives the best results. Follow the manufacturer's directions for applying fusible web to your fabric.

Thread

For piecing, use cotton thread in a neutral color, such as light gray or tan. For decorative machine stitching and quilting, use a decorative sewing-machine thread. Rayon thread has a nice sheen. For hand sewing and decorative stitching, such as making Yo-yos and embroidery, use perle cotton or embroidery floss. For hand quilting, use quilting thread or embroidery floss.

Needles

You need different needles for machine piecing, hand appliqué, embroidery, and hand quilting. I recommend size 80/12 needles for machine piecing, or try size 75/11 or 90/14 machine-quilting needles. The hole in the needle is a little larger, so the thread glides through easily. For hand appliqué, embroidery, and making Yo-yos, I recommend size 6 to 8 embroidery needles. Hand-quilting needles are called "Betweens." If you are a beginning quilter, you may want to experiment with different sizes to find which ones work best for you.

 **TIP**

Hand and machine needles are sized differently. For hand-stitching needles, the larger the number, the smaller the needle. For machine-stitching needles, the smaller the number, the smaller the needle.

Batting

For these projects, I recommend an 80/20 cotton-polyester batting. This type of batting is easy to machine quilt and lies flat when finished.

TOOLS

Sewing Machine

It's very important to keep your sewing machine in good working order. Clean and oil your machine regularly, after about sixty hours of sewing. Change your needle after every project; a sharp needle is better for the fabric. Finally, take your machine in for a "checkup" at least once a year.

Rotary Cutter and Cutting Mat

You need a rotary cutter and self-healing cutting mat for all the projects in this book. I like to place a rotary cutter and large cutting mat on my cutting table, and a smaller cutting mat next to my sewing machine. This way, I don't have to get up to trim my pieces and blocks. Always have a sharp blade in your rotary cutter.

Acrylic Rulers

There are many different acrylic cutting guides or rulers designed to work with rotary cutters. I recommend the 1" x 12", 6" x 24", 6" square, and 15" square rulers for these projects.

Scissors

You need a pair of sharp scissors for cutting out appliqué pieces. You may also want to keep a pair of small scissors by your sewing machine. These come in handy for snipping threads.

Iron and Ironing Board

Place a clean iron and ironing board or small pressing surface close to your sewing machine. I like using steam when I press.

You can make a small pressing surface. (Follow the instructions at right.) If you use one side of your pressing surface for pressing and the other side for fusible appliqué, you'll avoid having residue from the fusible web show up where you don't want it.

MAKING A PRESSING SURFACE

1. Ask your local hardware store to cut a 20" x 24" rectangle of soft-pressed board.
2. Wrap both sides of the board with Pellon fleece. Whipstitch the edges closed.
3. From 44"-wide muslin, cut a 26" x 44" rectangle.
4. Fold the muslin rectangle in half, right sides together, as shown. Stitch the side seams, then turn the muslin right side out.

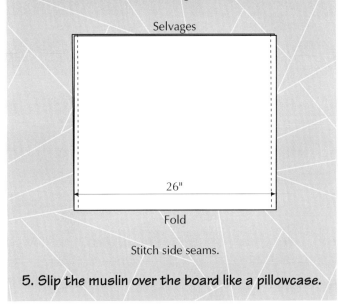

Selvages

26"

Fold

Stitch side seams.

5. Slip the muslin over the board like a pillowcase.

Miscellaneous Tools

You also need a fine-line permanent marker, seam ripper, tape measure, walking foot, darning foot, thimble, pencil, straight pins, and size 1 or 2 nickel-plated safety pins. A spray bottle filled with water is helpful for pressing stubborn seams.

The Quilter's Beginning Basics

The crazy patchwork projects in this book are easy to make when you use the following tips and techniques.

ROTARY CUTTING

Whether you are a beginner or advanced quiltmaker, always remember the following rules and tips for rotary cutting.

General rules:
- Close the blade on your rotary cutter every time you put it down.
- Keep your rotary cutter out of the reach of small children. The blades are very sharp.
- Cut away from yourself.

Rules for making these projects:
- Begin by squaring up your fabric.
- Cut strips on the crosswise grain.
- Cut the crazy patchwork pieces in any direction, making the best use of your fabric. Do not worry about the bias.
- Cut the border and binding strips first, then use the remaining fabric for the crazy patchwork and appliqué.

TIP

Measure twice; cut once!

THE PERFECT ¼" SEAM

An accurate ¼"-wide seam allowance is essential. If you don't have a ¼" foot for your sewing machine, measure and mark a seam guide on your machine. Put a piece of ¼" graph paper under the presser foot and lower the needle onto the graph paper, slightly to the right of the ¼" grid line. Put a piece of masking tape or moleskin along the edge of the graph paper.

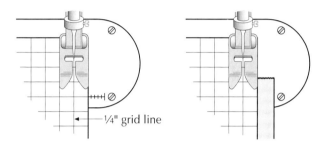

⅟₄" grid line

Use ¼" graph paper to locate a new seam guide.

TIP

Check your ¼"-wide seam allowance: Cut three 1¼" x 3" strips of fabric and sew them together, using your ¼" seam guide. Press. The center strip should measure 1" from seam to seam. If it doesn't, adjust the ¼" guide.

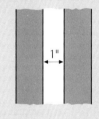

1"

PRESSING

For accurate patchwork, press as you sew! Press the seam flat to set the stitches, then use your iron to open the pieces and press the seam to one side. Do not press the seams in these projects open.

To prevent creases, always press from the right side of your quilt top.

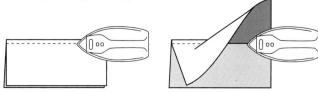

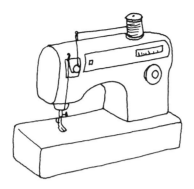

The Construction Techniques

Follow these easy construction techniques—freezer-paper piecing and fusible appliqué—for all the projects in this book.

CRAZY PATCHWORK

If you look at the patterns on the pullout, you'll notice that every piece is a different shape. This adds interest to the crazy patchwork. Don't worry—it's easier than it looks. Follow these basic steps for machine piecing the crazy patchwork blocks and borders. Read all the instructions before you begin, and have fun learning the technique.

To help you follow the crazy patchwork block patterns, I've used the following key.

– – – – Dashed lines divide the pattern into sections.
A, B, C Letters indicate sections.
1, 2, 3 The pieces are numbered sequentially for piecing.

1. Using a fine-line permanent marker, trace the crazy patchwork pattern onto a piece of tissue paper. Use this as your master pattern. Do not cut it apart.
2. Trace the pattern onto the dull side of a piece of freezer paper. (Remember, you press the shiny side to the fabric.) Be sure to label each piece.

3. Cut out the freezer-paper square, adding a ½"-wide seam allowance. Place the ½" mark on the ruler along the solid bold line. Cut along the edge of the ruler.

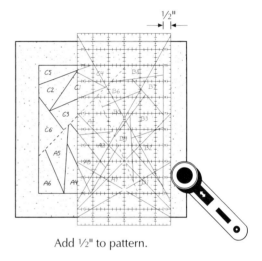

Add ½" to pattern.

4. Cut the sections apart along the dashed lines as shown.

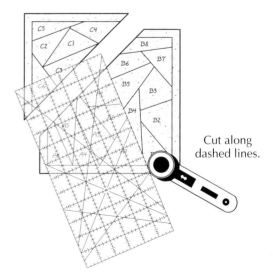

Cut along dashed lines.

5. Working with section A only, cut the pieces apart.

 TIP

> To avoid confusing or losing your freezer-pattern pieces, cut one section apart at a time. When cutting pieces, begin with the largest number and work downward.

6. Choose a piece of fabric to start your crazy patchwork. For best results, work with fabric pieces no larger than 6" x 22". Place pattern piece A1 on the wrong side of the fabric. Loosely cut around the template, leaving at least ¼" on all sides. Repeat until you have cut fabric for all pieces in the section. Place the pieces in a pile, with the largest number on top.

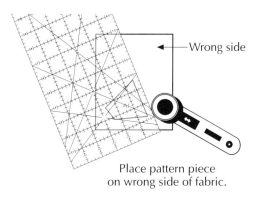

Place pattern piece
on wrong side of fabric.

7. Lightly press each freezer-pattern piece to the wrong side of the fabric pieces cut in step 6.
8. On pieces A1 and A2, trim accurate ¼"-wide seam allowances on the sides that will be joined. Refer to the master pattern made in step 1 for placement.

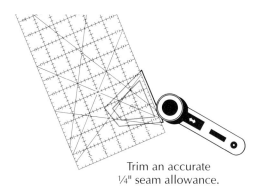

Trim an accurate
¼" seam allowance.

9. Place pieces A1 and A2 right sides together, with the larger number on top. Pin together at the corner of the freezer paper as shown. If you can't match the sides of the pattern pieces, make sure you have the right pieces turned in the correct direction.

Match corners of freezer paper.

10. Using the freezer paper as a seam guide, sew the pieces together. The freezer-paper pieces should match exactly, but it will not affect the overall appearance if your pieces are slightly different.

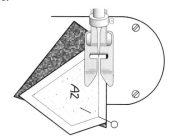

Use freezer paper as ¼" seam guide.

11. Press the seam toward the larger number. Remember to press as you sew.
12. Referring to the master pattern for placement, continue adding pieces until you complete the section. Do not remove the freezer paper until you have assembled the entire block or border. (The paper acts as a stabilizer, and you can use it to help keep track of what you're doing.)

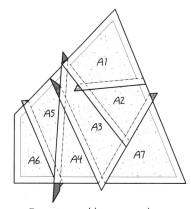

Press toward larger numbers.

13. Trim accurate ¼"-wide seam allowances on the sides that will be joined with other sections (the sides with dashed lines).

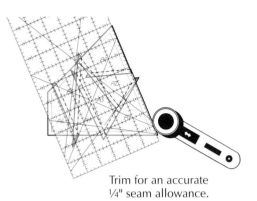

Trim for an accurate
¼" seam allowance.

14. Complete all the sections as described in steps 5–13.
15. Sew the sections together.

16. Using a 15" square acrylic ruler, trim the block to the size noted in the project.
17. Remove the freezer paper. You may need to gently tug on both sides of the seams to remove the paper from the stitches.

FUSIBLE APPLIQUÉ

The patterns on the pullout are reversed for fusible appliqué.

1. Place the fusible web, rough side down, on the pattern and trace. Use a pencil to trace the patterns onto fusible web.
2. Cut out the fusible web piece as shown, leaving about ¼" of webbing around the pattern piece.

MAKING YOUR OWN CRAZY PATCHWORK BLOCKS

1. Draw a square the desired size.
2. Divide the square into two or three sections with straight dashed lines.

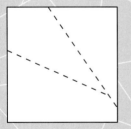

3. Working on one section at a time, draw the crazy patchwork pieces. Always connect two lines. Continue drawing until the section is complete.

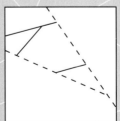

Always connect two lines.

4. Number the pieces, starting with 1. The next-number piece must not cover more than one side of the previous piece. Remember, you are numbering for assembly, so the numbers do not have to be placed sequentially. Refer to the illustration for ideas.

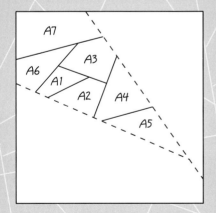

5. Repeat for the remaining sections.

3. Place the fusible web piece, rough side down, on the wrong side of the appliqué fabric. Following the manufacturer's directions, fuse the piece to the fabric. For best results, use a dry iron. Allow to cool.

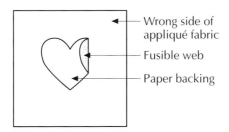

Wrong side of appliqué fabric
Fusible web
Paper backing

4. Cut out the appliqué piece on the drawn line and peel off the paper backing.
5. Position the appliqué piece on your background and fuse. I usually quilt and embroider my appliqués at the same time, after layering the backing, batting, and quilt top. Refer to the projects for quilting ideas.

EASIER, FASTER QUILTMAKING

Before you begin one of the projects, take a minute to set up your work space so you can work more efficiently. If you follow these tips, you won't have to get up from your sewing machine until you have finished the section.
• Place your iron to one side of your sewing machine, within reach.
• Set a small cutting mat, small ruler, rotary cutter, and scissors on the other side of your sewing machine.
• Keep the tissue-paper pattern handy so you can use it as a reference when placing the pieces.

The Projects

The crazy patchwork patterns and appliqué templates are provided on the pullout pattern. Before you begin, read all the instructions thoroughly, including "The Quilter's Beginning Basics" (page 9), "The Construction Techniques" (pages 10–13), and "The Finishing Touches" (pages 50–55). Remember the following tips as you work:

• Use an accurate ¼"-wide seam allowance.
• Following each step, press the seams in the direction of the arrows in the illustrations.
• Assemble the quilt top before fusing the appliqué pieces to the background.

For the Birds and the Bees

Color photo on page 25

FINISHED MEASUREMENTS

Quilt: 18" x 18"
Background Block: 11" x 11"
Inner Border: ½" wide
Crazy Patchwork Border: 3" wide

Materials: 44"-wide fabric

¼ yd. each of 10 different gold, green, blue, and pink prints for crazy patchwork blocks, appliqué pieces, and Yo-yos (or use scraps from your fabric stash)

½ yd. ivory print for background

¾ yd. red print for door, inner border, backing, and sleeve

¼ yd. dark blue print for binding

22" x 22" square of batting

½ yd. fusible web

1 yd. freezer paper

20 assorted buttons for flower centers

Embroidery floss

Cutting

*All measurements include
¼"-wide seam allowances.*

From the ivory print, cut:
1 square, 11½" x 11½", for background

From the red print, cut:
1 rectangle, 22" x 44", then cut into:
    1 square, 22" x 22", for backing
    2 strips, each 1" x 11½", for side inner borders
      (Refer to "Adding Borders" on pages 51–52.)
    2 strips, each 1" x 12½", for top and bottom inner
      borders
    1 strip 6" x 17", for quilt sleeve

From the dark blue print, cut:
2 strips, each 2¼" x 44", for binding

Making the Crazy Patchwork

*Refer to the basic construction technique in
"Crazy Patchwork" on pages 10–12.*

1. Using the 10" (finished) block pattern on the pull-out, make 2 blocks.
2. Trim one side of each block. From each block, cut 3 strips, each 3½" x 10½".

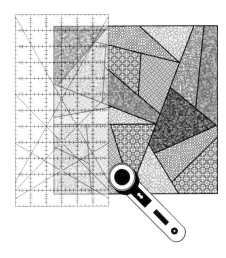

3. From the strips cut in step 2, cut 18 squares, each 3½" x 3½".
4. Using section 2 of the 10" (finished) block pattern, make 1 crazy patchwork strip. Trim to 3½" x 10½".
5. From the strip made in step 4, cut 2 squares, each 3½" x 3½".

6. Sew 4 crazy patchwork squares together for each side border.

Make 2.

7. Sew 6 crazy patchwork squares together for each of the top and bottom borders.

Make 2.

TIP

Arrange the crazy patchwork squares for the border on a design wall. You can move the blocks around until you are pleased with the layout.

Assembling the Quilt Top

1. Sew the 1" x 11½" inner border strips to the sides of the background block. Press toward the borders.
2. Sew the 1" x 12½" inner border strips to the top and bottom of the background block. Press toward the borders.
3. Sew the crazy patchwork borders made above to the sides, top, and bottom of the quilt top. Press toward the borders.

Adding the Appliqué Pieces

Refer to "Fusible Appliqué" on pages 12–13.

1. Using the templates on the pullout pattern, trace the appliqué pieces onto fusible web.
2. From a gold print, fuse and cut the birdhouse frame, door frame, and perch.
3. From a green print, fuse and cut the birdhouse roof, side, and front. Fuse and cut the flower leaves from assorted green prints.
4. From the red print, fuse and cut the birdhouse door.
5. From the blue prints, fuse and cut the birdhouse entry, bird body, flowerpot, flowerpot top, and pot stripes.
6. From a pink print, fuse and cut the bird wing.
7. Using fusible web, trace and cut 1 rectangle, 2¾" x 4", for the sign, and 1 strip, ½" x 3", for the stick. Fuse and cut the sign from a pink print, and the stick from a gold print.
8. Trace the lettering from the pullout pattern onto the flowerpot card.
9. Referring to the color photo on page 25 and the quilt diagram on page 14 for placement, fuse the appliqué pieces to the quilt top.

Finishing

Refer to "The Finishing Touches" on pages 50–55.

1. Layer the backing, batting, and quilt top.
2. Quilt and embroider as desired.
3. Using the templates on the pullout pattern, make 5 extra large, 7 large, 5 medium, and 4 small Yo-yos. Hand stitch the Yo-yos and buttons to the quilt top. See the color photo and quilt diagram for placement.
4. Add the name of your quilt, your signature, and the date to the bottom of the flowerpot card. Use a fine-line permanent marker or embroidery.

5. Make a sleeve and stitch it to the back of your quilt.
6. Bind the quilt.

Quilting Idea

CREATIVE INTERPRETATION

Everything Grows Better with Love

Color photo on page 25

Finished Measurements

Quilt: 15" x 23"

Crazy Patchwork Background: 8" x 16" (two 8" x 8" blocks)

Inner Border: 1" wide

Outer Border: 2½" wide

Stars for Wishes

Color photo on page 26

FINISHED MEASUREMENTS

Quilt: 19" x 29"
Crazy Patchwork Background: 10" x 20"
Crazy Patchwork Corner Blocks: 4" x 4"
Inner Border: 1" wide
Outer Border: 4" wide

Materials: 44"-wide fabric

¼ yd. each of 10 different blue prints for
crazy patchwork blocks (or use scraps
from your fabric stash)
Assorted gold, white, red, green, and
brown scraps for angel and stars
⅛ yd. gold print for stars
¼ yd. red print for inner border and bows
1⅛ yds. dark blue star print for
outer border, backing, and sleeve
¼ yd. red plaid for binding
23" x 33" rectangle of batting
7" x 7" square of batting
¼ yd. fusible web
1 yd. freezer paper
11 assorted buttons for embellishing stars
Embroidery floss

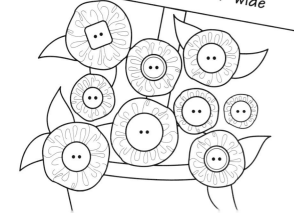

Cutting

*All measurements include
¼"-wide seam allowances.*

From the red print, cut:
3 strips, each 1½" x 44", then cut into:
    4 strips, each 1½" x 20½", for inner borders (Refer to "Adding Borders" on pages 51–52.)
    4 strips, each 1½" x 4½", for inner borders
From the dark blue star print, cut:
2 strips, each 4½" x 44", then cut into:
    2 strips, 4½" x 20½", for outer borders
    2 strips, 4½" x 10½", for outer borders
1 rectangle, 23" x 33", for backing
1 strip, 6" x 18", for quilt sleeve
From the red plaid, cut:
3 strips, each 2¼" x 44", for binding

Making the Crazy Patchwork

*Refer to the basic construction technique in
"Crazy Patchwork" on pages 10–12.*

1. Using the 10" (finished) block pattern on the pullout, make 2 blocks.
2. Trim the blocks to 10½" x 10½".
3. Join the blocks to make the 10½" x 20½" crazy patchwork background. You may want to rotate one block for a more random look.
4. Using the 4" (finished) block pattern on the pullout, make 4 crazy patchwork blocks. Trim the blocks to 4½" x 4½".

Assembling the Quilt Top

1. Sew the 1½" x 20½" inner border strips to the sides of the background block. Press toward the borders.

2. Sew the 4½" x 20½" outer border strips to the inner border strips. Press toward the inner borders.

3. Sew the 1½" x 20½" inner border strips to the top and bottom. Press toward the inner borders.
4. Sew a 1½" x 4½" inner border strip to each short side of a 4½" x 10½" outer border strip. Sew a 4½" x 4½" crazy patchwork block to each end. Press as shown. Repeat.

5. Sew the border made in step 4 to the top and bottom. Press toward the inner borders.

Adding the Appliqué Pieces

Refer to "Fusible Appliqué" on pages 12–13.
1. Using the templates on the pullout pattern, trace the appliqué pieces onto fusible web.
2. Fuse and cut the angel body, face, wings, halo, hands, legs, socks, shoes, and stars from the assorted scraps.
3. Using a fine-line permanent marker, trace the face. Embroider if desired.
4. Referring to the color photo on page 26 and the quilt diagram on page 17 for placement, fuse the appliqué pieces to the quilt top.

Finishing

Refer to "The Finishing Touches" on pages 50–55.

1. Layer the backing, batting, and quilt top.
2. Quilt and embroider as desired. An embroidery pattern for "Stars for Wishes" is provided on the pullout.
3. Using the template below right, make 5 small stars from the assorted scraps. Place the stars, right side up, on the 7" x 7" square of batting. Using embroidery floss, stitch around the edges of each star. (I use a running stitch.)

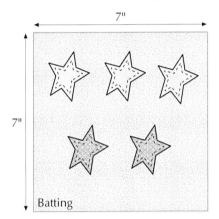

7"

7"

Batting

4. Cut out the stars. Referring to the color photo and quilt diagram for placement, arrange the stars around the angel and attach with embroidery floss and buttons. Finish by tying a knot on top and trimming the tails to ¼".

5. To make fabric bows, tear a 1" x 10" strip of red print. Tear this strip in six 1" x 1½" rectangles. Arrange the bows on the quilt, pinching the center of each. Attach with embroidery floss and buttons.

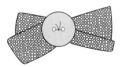

6. Make a label for your quilt.

7. Make a sleeve and stitch it to the back of your quilt.
8. Bind the quilt.

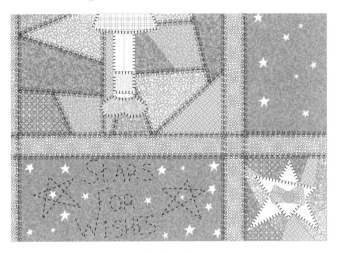

Quilting Idea

CREATIVE INTERPRETATION

Twinkle, Twinkle
Color photo on page 26

Finished Measurements
Quilt: 17" x 17"
Crazy Patchwork Background: 12" x 12"
(Nine 4" blocks)
Inner Border: ½" wide
Outer Border: 2" wide

Star
Cut 5

Love Notes

Materials: 44"-wide fabric

Directional fabrics are not recommended for this project.

1 yd. total of 10 different pink, rose, teal, and black prints for crazy patchwork blocks (or use scraps from your fabric stash)

¾ yd. pink print for background

1½ yds. burgundy print for baskets, inner border, backing, sleeve, and binding

¼ yd. teal print for accent triangles

25" x 44" rectangle of batting

4" x 4" square of batting

⅛ yd. fusible web

1⅓ yds. freezer paper

3 small handkerchiefs or doilies

1 yd. of 4mm silk ribbon

1 yd. of 7mm silk ribbon

1 heart charm

Embroidery floss

Color photo on page 30
FINISHED MEASUREMENTS
Quilt: 21¼" x 40"
Basket Blocks: 7½" x 7½", set diagonally
Inner Border: 1" wide
Crazy Patchwork Border: 3" wide

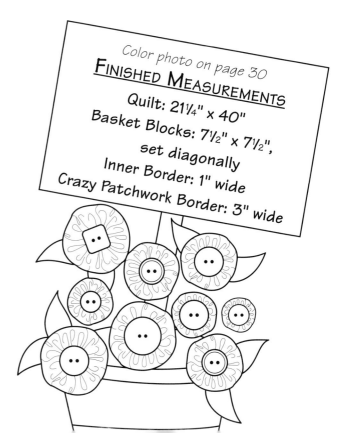

Cutting

*All measurements include
¼"-wide seam allowances.*

From the pink print, cut:
1 rectangle, 15½" x 44", then cut into:
    1 square, 15½" x 15½"
    2 squares, each 8" x 8"
    2 squares, each 5⅜" x 5⅜"
3 strips, each 2" x 44", then cut into:
    6 rectangles, each 2" x 5"
    30 squares, each 2" x 2"
From the burgundy print, cut:
1 strip, 5⅜" x 44", then cut into:
    2 squares, each 5⅜" x 5⅜"
    6 squares, each 2" x 2"
    1 strip, 3" x the remaining length, for basket
      handles
3 strips, each 1½" x 44", then cut into:
    2 strips, each 1½" x 32½", for side inner
      borders (Refer to"Adding Borders" on pages
      51–52.)
    2 strips, each 1½" x 15¾", for top and bottom
      inner borders
1 rectangle, 25" x 44", for backing
1 strip, 6" x 20", for quilt sleeve
4 strips, each 2¼" x 44", for binding
From the teal print, cut:
2 strips, each 2" x 44", then cut into:
    24 squares, each 2" x 2", for accent triangles
From each handkerchief or doily, cut a:
4¼" triangle (length of short sides) from decorated
    corner

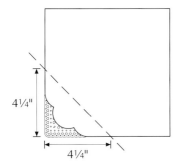

Making the Crazy Patchwork

*Refer to the basic construction technique in
"Crazy Patchwork" on pages 10–12.*

1. Using the 10" (finished) block pattern on the pull-out, make 4 blocks.
2. Trim one side of each block. From each block, cut 3 strips, each 3½" x 10½". See the illustration on page 15.
3. From the strips cut in step 2, cut 24 crazy patchwork rectangles, each 3½" x 4¾".
4. Using section 2 of the 10" (finished) block pattern, make 1 crazy patchwork strip. Trim to 3½" x 10½".
5. From the strip made in step 4, cut 2 crazy patchwork rectangles, each 3½" x 4¾".
6. Join 8 crazy patchwork squares for each side border.

Make 2.

7. Join 5 crazy patchwork rectangles for each of the top and bottom borders.

Assembling the Quilt Blocks

1. To make quick half-square triangle units, place pink and teal 2" squares right sides together. Stitch diagonally as shown. Trim ¼" from the seam line. Press toward the teal print. Make 24.

2. Repeat step 1, using pink and burgundy 2" squares. Make 6.
3. Using half-square triangles from step 1, make 3 of each unit as shown. Press as shown.

Make 3.

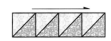

Make 3.

4. Using half-square triangle units from step 2 and 2" x 5" pink rectangles, make 3 units as shown. Press toward the rectangle.

Make 3.

5. Join 1 pink 2" x 5" rectangle, 1 pink and burgundy half-square triangle unit, and 1 pink and teal half-square triangle unit as shown. Make 3. Press toward the rectangle.

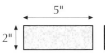   

Make 3.

6. Cut 2 burgundy 5⅜" squares in half diagonally. Set 1 triangle aside.

Cut 2.

7. Center a triangle cut from a handkerchief or doily, right sides together, on one of the basket triangles cut in step 6. Machine baste. Make 3. Set 1 aside.

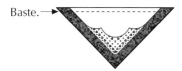

Make 3.

8. Cut 2 pink 5⅜" squares in half diagonally. Set 2 aside. Sew a pink triangle to 2 of the units made in step 7. Press toward the basket.

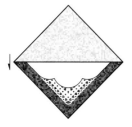

Make 2.

9. To make a pocket, join the pink triangles set aside in step 8 as shown.

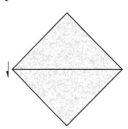

10. Sew the burgundy triangle set aside in step 6 to the handkerchief unit set aside in step 7, right sides together. Fold the handkerchief to the right side and press seam.

Press folded edge.

11. Place the basket pocket on top of the pink square made in step 8. Stitch the sides of the basket as shown.

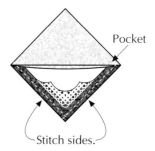

12. Assemble the block, working clockwise. Press as shown.

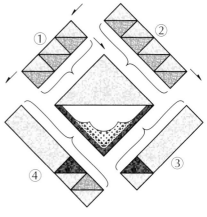

Make 3.

Assembling the Quilt Top

1. Cut the pink 15½" background square twice diagonally to make 4 side setting triangles.

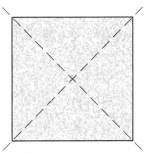

Side setting triangles

2. Sew the side setting triangles to the blocks as shown. Press toward the triangles, then trim the corners.

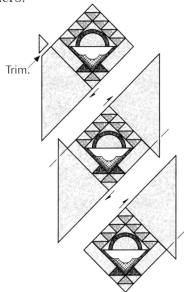

Trim.

Trim excess.

3. Join the rows as shown.

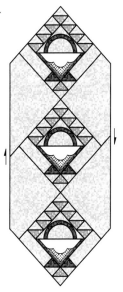

4. Cut 2 pink 8" squares in half diagonally to make 4 corner setting triangles.

Corner setting triangles

5. Mark the center of the Basket blocks and corner setting triangles as shown. Sew the corner setting triangles to the Basket blocks, matching the center points.

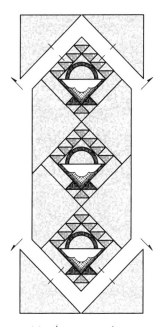

Match center points.

6. Trim the quilt-top center to 13¾" x 32½".
7. Sew the 1½" x 32½" inner border strips to the sides. Press toward the borders. ·
8. Sew the 1½" x 15¾" inner border strips to the top and bottom. Press toward the borders.
9. Sew the crazy patchwork borders to the sides, top, and bottom of the quilt top. Press toward the borders.

Adding the Appliqué Pieces

Refer to "Fusible Appliqué" on pages 12–13.

1. Using the template on the pullout pattern, trace 3 basket handles onto fusible web.
2. Fuse and cut the basket handles from the burgundy print.
3. Referring to the color photo on page 30 and the quilt diagram on page 20 for placement, fuse the basket handles to the quilt top.

Finishing

Refer to "The Finishing Touches" on pages 50–55.

1. Layer the backing, batting, and quilt top.
2. Quilt and embroider as desired.
3. Following the instructions in "Crazy Patchwork" on pages 10–12, make one 4" block.
4. Using the template on the pullout pattern, trace and cut 1 heart from the 4" block, backing, and 4" square of batting. Layer the crazy patchwork heart and backing, right sides together, with the batting sandwiched in between.
5. Sew around the heart, leaving a small opening for turning. Turn right side out and hand stitch the opening. Sign the heart as desired.
6. Using a 24"-long piece of 4mm silk ribbon, stitch around the heart, about ¼" from the edge. Tie the ends of the ribbon in a bow.
7. Cut an 18"-long piece of 7mm silk ribbon and tie a bow. Stitch the bow on one side of the bottom Basket block. Refer to the quilt photo on page 30 for placement. I used French knots (page 50) to attach the bow.

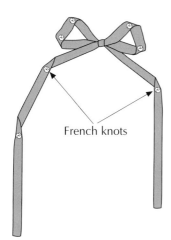

French knots

8. Tie the heart charm to one end of the ribbon. Attach the other end to the heart made in steps 3–6. Place the crazy heart in the basket if desired.
9. Make a sleeve and stitch it to the back of your quilt.
10. Bind the quilt.

Quilting Idea

CREATIVE INTERPRETATION

Legacy

Color photo on page 30

Finished Measurements
Quilt: 30" x 30"
Basket Block: 10" x 10"
Crazy Patchwork Corner Setting Triangles:
Two 10" x 10" blocks cut diagonally
Inner Border: 2"-wide ribbon border
Outer Border: 5" wide

Gallery

**For the Birds
and the Bees**

by Hollie Milne, 1996, Calgary, Alberta, Canada, 18" x 18". In this whimsical quilt, a birdhouse and a pot of Yo-yo flowers wait for the birds and the bees to come calling.

**Everything Grows
Better with Love**

by Hollie Milne, 1996, Calgary, Alberta, Canada, 15" x 23". This quilt features a romantic interpretation of the flower-pot in "For the Birds and the Bees."

Stars for Wishes

by Hollie Milne, 1996, Calgary, Alberta, Canada, 19" x 29". This angel would be adorable in Christmas colors or, if you are an angel collector like me, enjoy it all year 'round. This quilt has a country flavor.

Twinkle, Twinkle

by Ruth Walburger, 1996, Calgary, Alberta, Canada, 17" x 17". Ruth's quilt is a fun, fast, whimsical interpretation of "Stars for Wishes."

There Is No Place Like Home

by Hollie Milne, 1996, Calgary, Alberta, Canada, 22½" x 15". A transplanted American, I was inspired to create this patriotic quilt by thoughts of "the land of the free and the home of the brave."

Look Up at the Stars

by Hollie Milne, 1996, Calgary, Alberta, Canada, 18" x 18". Although this creative interpretation has a very different look than "There Is No Place Like Home," it still has a patriotic feel.

**He Loves Me,
He Loves Me Not**

by Hollie Milne, 1996, Calgary, Alberta, Canada, 18" x 24". This quilt brings back childhood memories of plucking the petals from daisies.

Everything's Coming Up Daisies

by Hollie Milne, 1996, Calgary, Alberta, Canada, 17½" x 13½". This place mat is a practical interpretation of "He Loves Me, He Loves Me Not."

Nurture Friendships

by Hollie Milne, 1996, Calgary, Alberta, Canada, 30" x 30". The fabric in this creative interpretation of "Spring Harvest" gives the quilt an old-fashioned mood.

Spring Harvest

by Hollie Milne, 1996, Calgary, Alberta, Canada, 26" x 26". Four darling watering cans sitting in the window are filled with the first flowers of spring.

Love Notes

by Hollie Milne, 1996,
Calgary, Alberta, Canada, 21¼" x 40".
A dramatic crazy patchwork border
surrounds three dainty baskets
accented with handkerchiefs. The
bottom basket is a pocket.

Legacy

by Hollie Milne, 1996,
Calgary, Alberta, Canada, 30" x 30".
This quilt has an old-fashioned,
nostalgic feeling.

Nesting Instinct

by Hollie Milne, 1996,
Calgary, Alberta, Canada, 43½" x 23½".
Four quaint birdhouses, arrayed in a row,
accent this quilt. If you look closely, you'll
find the birds that call them home.

Home on the Range

by Barbara Gibson, 1996,
Calgary, Alberta, Canada, 15½" x 23½".
This creative interpretation of "Nesting
Instinct" features a birdhouse for Country
Western fans.

'Tis the Season

by Hollie Milne, 1996, Calgary, Alberta, Canada, 38" x 48". This warm quilt features twelve delightful trees to decorate your home throughout the holiday season.

Around the Christmas Table

by Hollie Milne, 1996, Calgary, Alberta, Canada, 14" x 38". This table runner will add a festive touch to any holiday table.

He Loves Me, He Loves Me Not

Color photo on page 28

FINISHED MEASUREMENTS

Quilt: 18" x 24"
Crazy Patchwork Background: 10" x 14"
Inner Border: ½" wide
Middle Border: 1½" wide
Outer Border: 2" wide for sides,
3" wide for top and bottom

Materials: 44"-wide fabric

⅛ yd. each of 10 different blue prints for
crazy patchwork block (or use scraps
from your fabric stash)
Assorted gold, white, and green scraps
for flowers and stems
¼ yd. brown print for basket
1 yd. gold print for inner border, backing, and sleeve
⅛ yd. white print for middle border
½ yd. blue print for outer border and binding
22" x 28" rectangle of batting
½ yd. fusible web
½ yd. freezer paper
4 buttons, ¾" diameter, for flower centers
Embroidery floss

Cutting

*All measurements include
¼"-wide seam allowances.*

From the gold print, cut:
1 strip, 28" x 44", then cut into:
    1 rectangle, 28" x 22", for backing
    2 strips, each 1" x 14½", for side inner borders
    (Refer to "Adding Borders" on pages 51–52.)
    2 strips, each 1" x 11½", for top and bottom inner
    borders
    1 strip, 6" x 17", for quilt sleeve
From the white print, cut:
1 strip, 2" x 44", then cut into:
    2 strips, each 2" x 15½", for side middle borders
    2 strips, each 2" x 14½", for top and bottom middle
    borders
From the blue print, cut:
1 strip, 2½" x 44", then cut into:
    2 strips, each 2½" x 18½", for side outer bor-
    ders
1 strip, 3½" x 44", then cut into:
    2 strips, each 3½" x 18½", for top and bottom
    outer borders
3 strips, each 2¼" x 44", for binding

Making the Crazy Patchwork

*Refer to the basic construction technique in
"Crazy Patchwork" on pages 10–12.*

1. Using section 1 of the 10" (finished) block pattern on the pullout, make 2 blocks.
2. Trim the blocks to 7½" x 10½".
3. Join the blocks to make a 10½" x 14½" crazy
patchwork background. You may want to rotate
one block for a more random look.

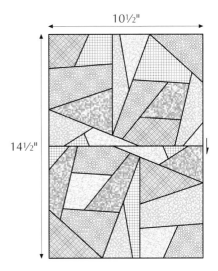

Assembling the Quilt Top

1. Sew the 1" x 14½" inner border strips to the
sides of the background block. Press toward the
borders, then sew the 1" x 11½" inner border
strips to the top and bottom. Press toward the
borders.
2. Sew the 2" x 15½" middle border strips to the
sides. Press toward the middle borders, then sew
the 2" x 14½" middle border strips to the top
and bottom. Press toward the middle borders.
3. Sew the 2½" x 18½" outer border strips to the
sides. Press toward the outer borders, then sew
the 3½" x 18½" outer border strips to the top
and bottom. Press toward the outer borders.

Adding the Appliqué Pieces

Refer to "Fusible Appliqué" on pages 12–13.

1. Using the templates on the pullout pattern, trace
the appliqué pieces onto fusible web.
2. Fuse and cut the basket, flowers, stems, and
leaves from the basket fabric and assorted scraps.
3. Referring to the color photo on page 28 and the
quilt diagram on page 33 for placement, fuse
the appliqué pieces to the quilt top.

Finishing

Refer to "The Finishing Touches" on pages 50–55.

1. Layer the backing, batting, and quilt top.
2. Quilt and embroider as desired. An embroidery
pattern for "He Loves Me, He Loves Me Not" is
provided on the pullout. Remember to sign and
date your quilt.
3. Using embroidery floss, stitch buttons for the
flower centers. Finish by tying a knot on the top
and trimming the tails to ¼".
4. Make a sleeve and stitch it to the back of your
quilt.
5. Bind the quilt.

Quilting Idea

CREATIVE
INTERPRETATION

Everything's Coming Up Daisies (place mat)

Color photo on page 28

Finished Measurements

Quilt: 17½" x 13½"

Crazy Patchwork Background: 10" x 10"

Appliqué Block: 4" x 10"

Border: 1¾" wide

There Is No Place Like Home

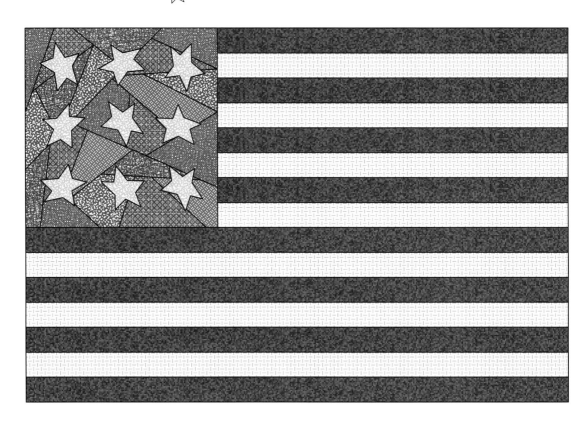

Color photo on page 27

FINISHED MEASUREMENTS

Quilt: 22½" x 15"

Crazy Patchwork Block: 8" x 8"

Stripes: 1" wide

Materials: 44"-wide fabric

Directional fabrics are not recommended for this project.
⅛ yd. each of 8 different blue prints for crazy patchwork (or use scraps from your fabric stash)
⅛ yd. gold print (or 9" x 9" square) for stars
¼ yd. red print for stripes
¼ yd. beige print for stripes
1¼ yds. blue print for backing, sleeve, and binding
19" x 26" rectangle of batting
⅛ yd. fusible web (or 9" x 9" square)
⅛ yd. freezer paper (or 10" x 10" square)
Embroidery floss

Cutting

*All measurements include
¼"-wide seam allowances.*

From the red print, cut:
4 strips, each 1½" x 44", then cut *each* strip into:
    1 strip, each 1½" x 15", for short stripes
    1 strip, each 1½" x 23", for long stripes

From the beige print, cut:
4 strips, each 1½" x 44", then cut *each* strip into:
    1 strip, each 1½" x 15", for short stripes
    1 strip, each 1½" x 23", for long stripes

From the blue print, cut:
1 rectangle, 26" x 19", for backing
1 strip, 6" x 21½", for quilt sleeve
2 strips, each 2¼" x 44", for binding

Making the Crazy Patchwork

*Refer to the basic construction technique in
"Crazy Patchwork" on pages 10–12.*

1. Using the 8" (finished) block pattern on the pull-out, make 1 block.
2. Trim the block to 8½" x 8½".

Assembling the Quilt Top

1. Sew the short red and beige stripes together as shown. Press toward the red stripes.

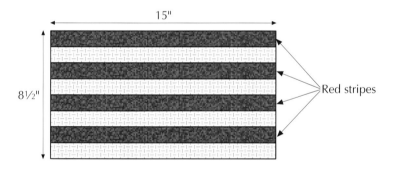

2. Sew the striped unit made in step 1 to the crazy patchwork block. Press toward the block.

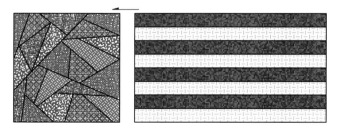

3. Sew the long red and beige stripes together as shown. Press toward the red stripes.

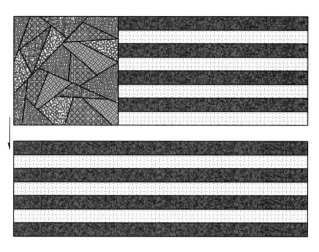

Adding the Appliqué Pieces

Refer to "Fusible Appliqué" on pages 12–13.

1. Using the template below, trace 9 stars onto fusible web.
2. Fuse and cut the stars from the gold print.
3. Referring to the color photo on page 27 and the quilt diagram on facing page for placement, fuse the stars to the quilt top.

Star
Cut 9

Finishing

Refer to "The Finishing Touches" on pages 50–55.

1. Layer the backing, batting, and quilt top.
2. Quilt and embroider as desired. There is no embroidery pattern for "There Is No Place Like Home." I used machine embroidery to include the name of my quilt, my name, and the date in the bottom beige stripe. You can use machine embroidery or hand embroidery to sign and date your quilt.
3. Make a sleeve and stitch it to the back of your quilt.
4. Bind the quilt.

Quilting Idea

CREATIVE INTERPRETATION

Look Up at the Stars
Color photo on page 27

Finished Measurements
Quilt: 18" x 18"
Crazy Patchwork Background: 8" x 8"
Inner Border: 1" wide
Middle Border: 2"-wide checkerboard
Outer Border: 2" wide

Spring Harvest

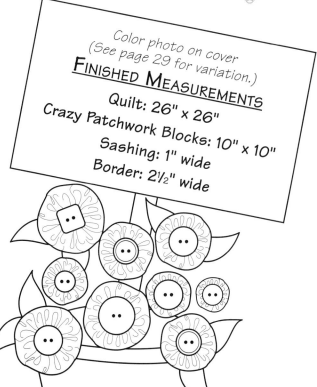

Color photo on cover
(See page 29 for variation.)

FINISHED MEASUREMENTS

Quilt: 26" x 26"

Crazy Patchwork Blocks: 10" x 10"

Sashing: 1" wide

Border: 2½" wide

Materials: 44"-wide fabric

1 yd. total of 8 different white prints
for crazy patchwork blocks

¼ yd. each of 5 blue prints for watering
cans (or 6" x 12" pieces)

Assorted yellow and green scraps
for Yo-yo flowers and leaves

1¾ yds. blue print for sashing, border,
backing, sleeve, and binding

30" x 30" square of batting

3½" x 5" rectangle of batting

1 yd. fusible web

1⅓ yds. freezer paper

10"-square handkerchief with lace edging

25 assorted buttons for flower centers

Embroidery floss

Cutting

All measurements include
¼"-wide seam allowances.

From the blue print, cut:
1 strip, 1½" x 44", then cut into:
   2 strips, each 1½" x 10½", for vertical sashing
   1 strip, 1½" x 21½", for horizontal sashing
3 strips, each 3" x 44", then cut into:
   2 strips, each 3" x 21½", for side borders (Refer
     to "Adding Borders" on pages 51–52.)
   2 strips, each 3" x 26½", for top and bottom
     borders
1 rectangle, 30" x 44", then cut into:
   1 rectangle, 30" x 30", for backing
   1 strip, 6" x 25", for quilt sleeve
3 strips, each 2¼" x 44", for binding
1 rectangle, 3½" x 5", for label backing
2 strips, each ¾" x 3", for label side borders
2 strips, each ¾" x 5", for label top and bottom
   borders
From the handkerchief, cut a:
4½" triangle (length of short sides) from each corner

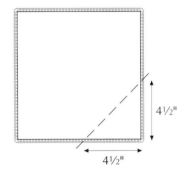

Making the Crazy Patchwork

Refer to the basic construction technique in
"Crazy Patchwork" on pages 10–12.
1. Using the 10" (finished) block pattern on the pullout, make 4 blocks.
2. Trim the blocks to 10½" x 10½".

Assembling the Quilt Top

1. With right sides together, place a handkerchief corner in the center bottom of a crazy patchwork block. Using a ¼"-wide seam allowance, machine baste. Repeat for all 4 blocks. Rotate the blocks for a random look.

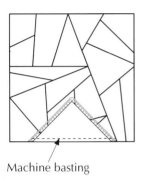

Machine basting

2. Join 2 blocks with a 1½" x 10½" sashing strip as shown. Press toward the sashing strip. Repeat.

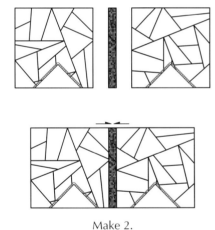

Make 2.

3. Join the block units made in step 2 with a 1½" x 21½" sashing strip. Press toward the sashing strip.

4. Sew the 3" x 21½" border strips to the sides. Press toward the borders.
5. Sew the 3" x 26½" border strips to the top and bottom. Press toward the borders.

Adding the Appliqué Pieces

Refer to "Fusible Appliqué" on pages 12–13.

1. Using the templates on the pullout pattern, trace the appliqué pieces onto fusible web.
2. Fuse and cut the watering-can pieces and leaves from the blue and green prints.
3. Referring to the color photo on the cover and the quilt diagram on page 39 for placement, fuse the watering-can pieces and leaves to the quilt top.

Finishing

Refer to "The Finishing Touches" on pages 50–55.

1. Layer the backing, batting, and quilt top.
2. Quilt and embroider as desired.
3. Using the templates on the pullout pattern, make 5 extra large, 7 large, 3 medium, and 5 small Yo-yos. Hand stitch the Yo-yos and buttons to the quilt top. See the color photo and quilt diagram for placement. Stitch a few extra buttons among the Yo-yos for flowers.
4. To make a card label, cut one 3" x 4½" rectangle from any white print. Sew the ¾" x 3" strips to the label sides. Sew the ¾" x 5" strips to the label top and bottom. Layer the label front and 3½" x 5" backing, right sides together, with a 3½" x 5" piece of batting sandwiched in between.
5. Sew around the label, leaving a 2"-wide opening for turning. Turn right side out and hand stitch the opening closed. Quilt around the border.

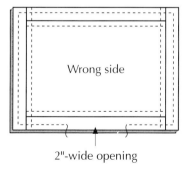

Wrong side

2"-wide opening

6. Using a fine-line permanent marker or embroidery, add the name of the quilt, your signature, and the date to the label.
7. Attach the label under the Yo-yo flowers on the lower left block.
8. Make a sleeve and stitch it to the back of your quilt.
9. Bind the quilt.

Quilting Idea

CREATIVE INTERPRETATION

Nurture Friendships
Color photo on page 29

Finished Measurements
Quilt: 30" x 30"
Crazy Patchwork Background: 10" x 10"
First Border: 1" wide
Second Border: 1½" wide
Third Border: 2"-wide checkerboard
Fourth Border: 3"-wide pieced with Ninepatch corner blocks
Fifth border: 3" wide

Nesting Instinct

Color photo on page 31

FINISHED MEASUREMENTS

Quilt: 43½" x 23½"

Crazy Patchwork Background: 10" x 30"

Inner Border: 4" wide

Middle Border: 2" wide (flying-geese units)

Outer Border: ¾" wide

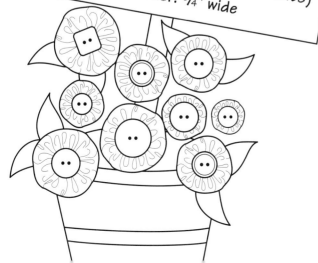

Materials: 44"-wide fabric

½ yd. total of 10 different green prints for crazy patchwork blocks (or use scraps from your fabric stash)

Assorted beige, blue, pink, brown, and white scraps for birdhouses, birds, bird's nest, tree limb, and leaves

1 yd. beige print for borders

⅓ yd. blue print for flying-geese units

2 yds. pink print for backing, sleeve, cornerstones, and binding

28" x 48" rectangle of batting

1 yd. fusible web

1 yd. freezer paper

8"-round lace doily

6"-square lace doily

Cutting

*All measurements include
¼"-wide seam allowances.*

From the beige print, cut:
3 strips, each 4½" x 44", then cut into:
    2 strips, each 4½" x 18½", for side inner borders (Refer to "Adding Borders" on pages 51–52.)
    2 strips, each 4½" x 30½", for top and bottom inner borders
8 strips, each 1½" x 44", then cut into:
    224 squares, each 1½" x 1½", for flying-geese units
4 strips, each 1¼" x 44", then cut into:
    2 strips, each 1¼" x 24", for outer side borders
    2 strips, each 1¼" x 42½", for outer top and bottom borders

From the blue print, cut:
4 strips, each 2½" x 44", then cut into:
    112 rectangles, each 1½" x 2½", for flying-geese units

From the pink print, cut:
1 rectangle, 44" x 48" (cut lengthwise), then cut into:
    1 rectangle, 28" x 48" (cut lengthwise), for backing
    1 strip, 6" x 42½", for sleeve
    4 squares, each 2½" x 2½", for cornerstones
4 strips, each 2¼" x 44", for binding

Making the Crazy Patchwork

*Refer to the basic construction technique in
"Crazy Patchwork" on pages 10–12.*

1. Using the 10" (finished) block pattern on the pullout, make 3 blocks.
2. Trim the blocks to 10½" x 10½".
3. Join the blocks to make the 10½" x 30½" crazy patchwork background. You may want to rotate the blocks for a more random look.

Assembling the Quilt Top

1. To make a flying-geese unit, place a beige 1½" square on a blue 1½" x 2½" rectangle, right sides together, as shown. Stitch across the diagonal of the square. Fold and press the square. Make 112.

Stitch.   Fold and press.

2. To complete the flying-geese unit, place a beige 1½" square on the other side of a blue 1½" x 2½" rectangle, right sides together, as shown. Stitch across the diagonal of the square. Fold and press the square. Make 112 flying-geese units.

Stitch.   Fold and press.

3. Join 19 flying-geese units. Make 4 sets. For sharp points, turn the unit over and sew directly through the point where the two lines intersect.

¼" seam allowance
where seams intersect

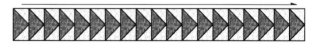

Press toward flying-geese units.

 TIP

Use the pink rectangle as a stitching guide when joining units, adjusting so any shortage is in the seam allowance.

4. Join 2 of the flying-geese sets made in step 3 as shown. Press the seams open. Make 2 for the top and bottom flying-geese borders.

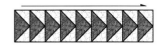

5. Join 9 flying-geese units. Make 4 sets.

Press toward flying-geese units.

6. Join 2 of the flying-geese units made in step 5 as shown. Sew a pink 2½" square to each end for cornerstones. Make 2 for the side flying-geese borders.

7. Cut the 6"-square and 8"-round doily in half. Using a ¼"-wide seam allowance, machine baste half of each, right sides together, to the background block as shown.

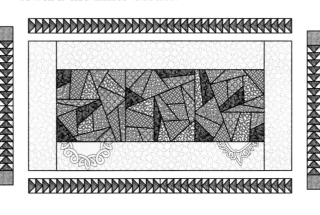

Baste doilies to bottom of crazy patch blocks.

8. Sew the 4½" x 30½" beige strips to the top and bottom. Press toward the borders.
9. Sew the 4½" x 18½" beige strips to the sides. Press toward the borders.
10. Sew the flying-geese borders to the top and bottom. Press toward the inner border.
11. Sew the flying-geese borders to the sides. Press toward the inner border.

12. Sew the 1¼" x 24" outer border strips to the sides. Press toward the outer borders, then sew the 1¼" x 42½" outer border strips to the top and bottom. Press toward the outer borders.

Adding the Appliqué Pieces

Refer to "Fusible Appliqué" on pages 12–13.

1. Using the templates on the pullout and on page 45, trace the appliqué pieces onto fusible web.
2. Fuse and cut the birdhouses, birds, bird's nest, tree limb, and leaves from the assorted beige, blue, pink, brown, and white scraps.
3. Referring to the color photo on page 31 and the quilt diagram on page 42 for placement, fuse the pieces to the quilt top.

Finishing

Refer to "The Finishing Touches" on pages 50–55.

1. Layer the backing, batting, and quilt top.
2. Quilt as desired.
3. Make a label for your quilt.
4. Make a sleeve and stitch it to the back of your quilt.
5. Bind the quilt.

Quilting Idea

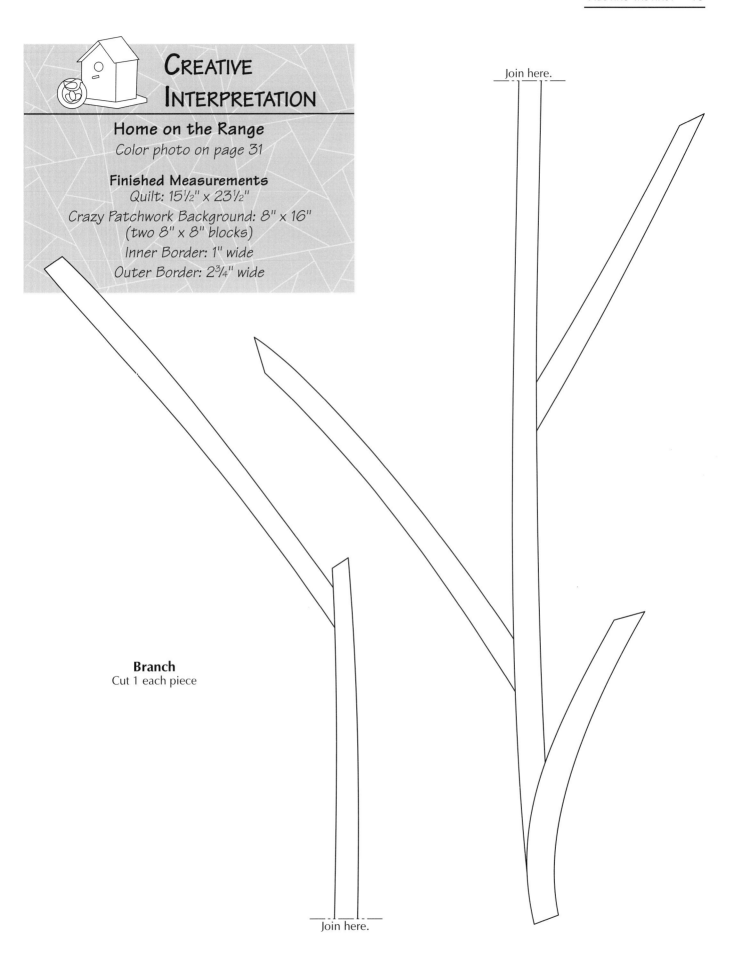

CREATIVE INTERPRETATION

Home on the Range
Color photo on page 31

Finished Measurements
Quilt: 15½" x 23½"
Crazy Patchwork Background: 8" x 16"
(two 8" x 8" blocks)
Inner Border: 1" wide
Outer Border: 2¾" wide

Join here.

Branch
Cut 1 each piece

Join here.

'Tis the Season

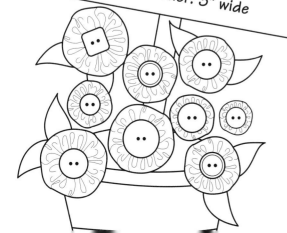

Color photo on page 32

FINISHED MEASUREMENTS

Quilt: 38" x 48"

Crazy Patchwork Block: 8" x 8"

Sashing: 2" wide

Inner Border with Quick-Pieced Stars: 4" wide

Outer Border: 3" wide

Materials: 44"-wide fabric

Directional fabrics are not recommended for this project.

2 yds. total of 8 different cream prints for crazy patchwork blocks (or use scraps from your fabric stash)

¼ yd. gold print for stars (or ⅛ yd. each of 2 different gold prints)

¾ yd. green print for sashing, trees, and binding

2¼ yds. red print for sashing, planter rims, backing, and sleeve

⅝ yd. red check for tree pots and borders

42" x 52" rectangle of batting

1 yd. fusible web

2 yds. freezer paper

Cutting

All measurements include
¼"-wide seam allowances.

From the gold print, cut:
1 strip, 2½" x 44", then cut into:
    10 squares, each 2½" x 2½", for star centers
3 strips, each 1½" x 4", then cut into:
    64 squares, each 1½" x 1½", for star points

From the green print, cut:
8 strips, each 1" x 44", then cut into:
    17 strips, each 1" x 8½", for inner sashing
    2 strips, each 1" x 38½", for side sashing
    2 strips, each 1" x 28½", for top and bottom
        sashing
4 strips, each 2¼" x 44", for binding

From the red print, cut:
14 strips, each 1¼" x 44", then cut into:
    34 strips, each 1¼" x 8½", for inner sashing
    4 strips, each 1¼" x 38½", for side sashing
    4 strips, each 1¼" x 28½", for top and bottom
        sashing
1 rectangle, 44" x 52" (cut lengthwise), for backing
1 strip, 6" x 37", for quilt sleeve

From the red check, cut:
4 strips, each 3½" x 44", then cut into:
    2 strips, each 3½" x 42½", for side borders
        (Refer to "Adding Borders" on pages 51–52.)
    2 strips, each 3½" x 38½", for top and bottom
        borders

Making the Crazy Patchwork

Refer to the basic construction technique in
"Crazy Patchwork" on pages 10–12.

1. Using the 8" (finished) block pattern on the pull-
    out, make 12 blocks.
2. Trim the blocks to 8½" x 8½".

Assembling the Quilt Top

1. To make the inner sashing, sew a 1¼" x 8½" red
    sashing strip on each side of a 1" x 8½" green
    sashing strip. Press toward red strips. Make 17.

2. To make the star points, place a 1½" gold square,
    right sides together, on one end of the sashing
    units made in step 1 as shown. Sew across the
    diagonal of the square. Fold and press the square.
    Repeat for the remaining 16 sashing units.

Stitch.   Fold and
                 press.

3. Sew a 1½" gold square, right sides together, on
    the other end of the sashing units as shown.
    Sew across the diagonal of the square. Fold and
    press the square. Repeat for the remaining 16
    sashing units. Set 10 sashing units aside.

Stitch.   Fold and
                 press.

4. Following the instructions in steps 2 and 3, sew star points on the opposite ends of 7 sashing units as shown.

Make 7.

5. To make the side sashing, sew a 1¼" x 38½" red sashing strip on each side of a 1" x 38½" green sashing strip. Press toward the red strips. Make 2. Following the instructions in steps 2 and 3, sew star points to both ends of the sashing units.

6. To make the top and bottom sashing, repeat step 5, using the 1¼" x 28½" red sashing strips and 1" x 28½" green sashing strips.

7. Assemble the crazy patchwork blocks, sashing units, and star centers as shown. Press toward the border and star centers. You may want to rotate the crazy patchwork blocks for a more random look.

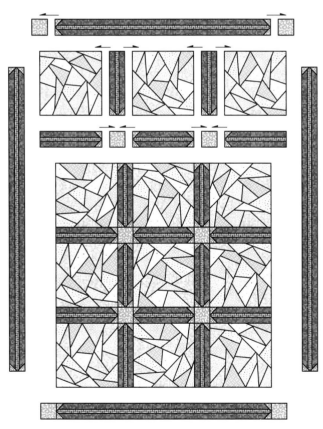

Assembly Diagram

8. Sew the 3½" x 42½" red check border strips to the sides. Press toward the borders.

9. Sew the 3½" x 38½" red check border strips to the top and bottom. Press toward the borders.

Adding the Appliqué Pieces

Refer to "Fusible Appliqué" on pages 12–13.

1. To make the trees, cut 1 strip, 9" x 22", from fusible web and fuse to the green print. From this, cut 18 strips, each ½" x 22". Then cut branches for the trees as follows:

   12 pieces, each ½" x 6½"
   12 pieces, each ½" x 6"
   12 pieces, each ½" x 5"
   12 pieces, each ½" x 4"
   12 pieces, each ½" x 3"
   12 pieces, each ½" x 2"

2. To make the tree pots, cut 1 strip, 4" x 12", from the fusible web and fuse to the red check. From this, cut 2 strips, each 2" x 12". Cut the strips into 12 squares, each 2" x 2".

3. To make the tree-pot rims, cut 1 strip, 1" x 15", from fusible web and fuse to the red print. From this, cut 12 rectangles, each ½" x 2½".

4. Using the template below, trace 12 stars onto fusible web. Fuse and cut the stars from the gold print.

5. Referring to the color photo on page 32 and the quilt diagram on page 46 for placement, fuse the appliqué pieces to the quilt top.

Finishing

Refer to "The Finishing Touches" on pages 50–55.

1. Layer the backing, batting, and quilt top.
2. Quilt as desired.
3. Make a label for your quilt.
4. Make a sleeve and stitch it to the back of your quilt.
5. Bind the quilt.

Star
Cut 12

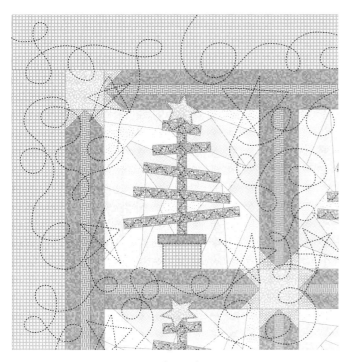

Quilting Idea

CREATIVE INTERPRETATION

Around the Christmas Table (table runner)

Color photo on page 32

Finished Measurements
Quilt: 14" x 38"
Crazy Patchwork Backgrounds:
Two 8" x 8" blocks
Scrap-Pieced Stars: 4" x 4"
Inner Border: ½" wide
Outer Border: 2½" wide

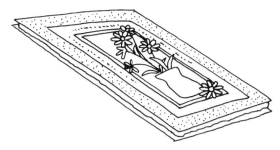

The Finishing Touches

Use the instructions in this section for embroidery stitches, making Yo-yos, preparing the quilt for quilting, quilting methods, making a sleeve, binding the quilt, and making a label.

EMBROIDERY STITCHES

You can use machine or hand embroidery for the quilts in this book. If you choose to hand embroider, remember:

- Stitch after you have layered the quilt, being careful not to go through the backing.
- Use a hoop to keep the fabric smooth.
- Use perle cotton or two strands of embroidery floss.
- Use the smallest comfortable needle.
- Keep your thread length no longer than 18".
- Begin and end embroidery as you would hand quilting (see page 53).
- It's better for your stitches to be even than small.

Buttonhole or Blanket Stitch

Bring the needle up at A. Holding the thread under your left thumb, bring the needle down at B and back up at C. To add interest, try stitching with two different-colored threads.

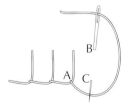

Chain Stitch

Bring the needle up at A. Leave a small loop of thread as you bring the needle back down at A. Pass the needle through the loop and bring it up at B.

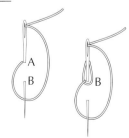

Chevron Stitch

Bring the needle up at A, down at B, and up at C as shown.

French Knot

Bring the needle up from the back at A. Wrap the thread around the needle twice as shown. Bring the needle down as close to A as possible. Using your thumbnail, hold the wraps on the needle until you pull it though.

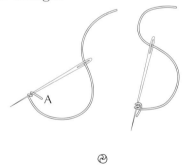

Lazy Daisy Stitch

Work this stitch the same as a chain stitch (see above), but fasten each loop with a small tack stitch as shown. You can work this stitch singly or in groups.

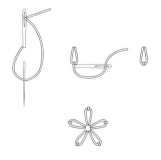

Stem Stitch

Bring the needle up at A, down at B, and up at C as shown, then bring the needle down at D and up at B.

MAKING YO-YOS

1. Using the patterns on the pullout, trace a Yo-yo the desired size on freezer paper. Cut out the freezer-paper template.
2. Press the template onto fabric, then cut out the Yo-yo. You can layer pieces of fabric to make several Yo-yos at a time. Remove the paper template.
3. Thread a needle with a 20"-long strand of perle cotton or several strands of embroidery floss. Make a knot about 4" from the end.
4. With the wrong side of the fabric facing you, fold over ¼" and stitch as shown. Use a running stitch; stitches should be about ¼" long. Stitch around the folded edge of the Yo-yo, gathering the thread against the knot.

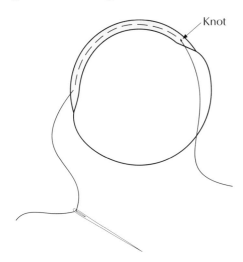

Knot

5. When you have stitched completely around the Yo-yo, distribute the stitches and flatten the Yo-yo. The hole in the center should be about the size of your pinkie finger.

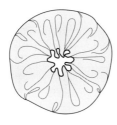

6. Tie the tails in a knot. Do not remove the needle or trim the tails.
7. Place the Yo-yo on a background, gathered side up. Take one stitch through the Yo-yo and quilt top.
8. Stitch a button in the middle of the Yo-yo, being careful not to stitch through the quilt. Knot the thread tails on top, then trim.

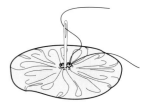

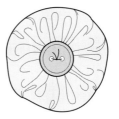

ADDING BORDERS

You may want to wait until you have pieced the center of your quilt top before cutting borders. Quilts must be sewn accurately, with a perfect ¼" seam, to fit together as planned. Measure, cut, and sew borders as follows.

1. Measure the quilt top through the center, top to bottom, to determine the length of the side borders. If your measurements are different from those in the projects, cut border strips according to your measurements and stitch. Press toward the border strips.

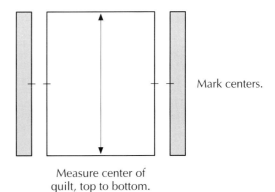

Mark centers.

Measure center of quilt, top to bottom.

2. Measure the quilt top through the center, side to side including borders, to determine the length of the top and bottom borders. Cut border strips that size and stitch. Press toward the border strips.

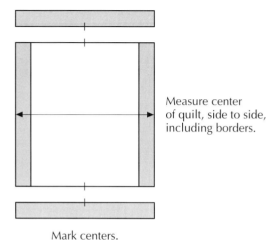

Measure center
of quilt, side to side,
including borders.

Mark centers.

MARKING THE QUILT TOP

The quilts pictured in this book were free-motion machine quilted, so there are quilting ideas but no patterns. You may want to mark a diamond pattern or, for more interesting designs, look for stencils at your local quilt shop.

When you mark a quilting pattern on the quilt top, choose a pencil or marker you can see, one that easily brushes, erases, or washes away. I use a gray quilter's pencil for marking my quilt tops.

Mark the quilt top before layering, using as fine a line as possible.

LAYERING THE QUILT

1. Cut the backing and batting 2" to 4" larger than the quilt top.
2. Lay the backing, right side down, on a large work table or floor. Secure the edges with masking tape.
3. Center the batting and quilt top, right side up, on the backing.

4. Beginning in the center, baste the quilt with safety pins. Place pins every 3" to 4" as shown.

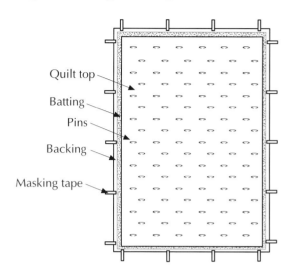

Quilt top
Batting
Pins
Backing
Masking tape

To prevent sore fingers, place the edge of a grapefruit spoon firmly against the quilt where you are going to pin. Place the pin in the quilt like a straight pin. Close the safety pin, using the serrated edge of the spoon to push the point into the clasp.

QUILTING

The quilts in this book were machine quilted, but I encourage you to hand embroider and quilt your projects if you wish (and if you have time). I've included some basic instructions for both methods to help you get started. Look at the projects for quilting ideas.

When I machine quilt, I use decorative stitches to embroider the crazy patchwork and quilt at the same time. Choosing a variety of different decorative stitches adds to the charm of the quilt.

Machine Quilting

For best results, use a walking foot for straight lines and a darning foot for free-motion quilting.

Walking foot   Darning foot

1. Begin by bringing the bobbin thread up to the top of the quilt.
2. Make a few stitches with the stitch length set at 0. This will secure the quilting stitches. Reset the stitch length and continue stitching.
3. For stippling or free-motion machine quilting, disengage the feed dogs of your machine. Guide the quilt under the needle with both hands, working at an even pace so the stitches will be consistent in length.

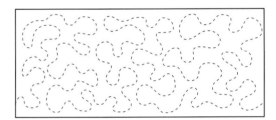

Stippling

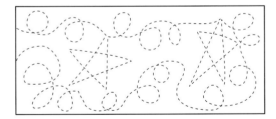

Free-motion swirls and stars

4. To end a line of quilting, return the stitch length to 0 and stitch. Cut the thread on the top and bottom of the quilt.
5. Using your rotary-cutting equipment, trim excess batting and backing even with the quilt top.

Hand Quilting

These projects can easily be quilted in your lap, and they are portable enough to take along when you are on the go.

1. Place the basted quilt in a quilting hoop. Do not use an embroidery hoop.
2. Cut an 18"-long piece of quilting thread and tie a knot at one end.
3. Begin quilting in the center of the quilt. Insert the needle in the top layer of your quilt about ½" from where you want to begin quilting. Bring your needle up at your beginning point and give a slight tug to bury the knot inside the batting.

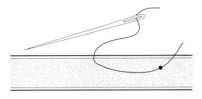

Gently pop knot into batting.

4. Rock the needle back and forth through all layers. Make small, even stitches, trying to get 3 to 4 stitches on your needle at once. Remember, it is more important for your stitches to be even than small.

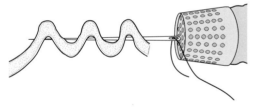

5. When you come to the end of your thread or a line of stitching, make a knot close to the quilt top. Insert the needle through the top fabric and batting at the base of the knot, popping the knot into the batting.

6. Bring your needle up through the quilt top and clip the thread close to the surface.
7. Trim the excess batting and backing even with the quilt top.

Making a Sleeve

Always add a hanging sleeve to your quilt. Push the sleeve up a little before blind stitching. This keeps the rod from straining the backing.

1. Cut a 6"-wide strip of fabric 1" shorter than the quilt width.
2. Fold in half lengthwise, right sides together. Stitch the short ends, then turn right side out.

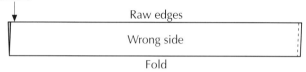

3. Pin the raw edge of the sleeve to the top raw edge of the quilt. Stitch.

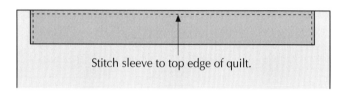

4. After attaching the binding, blindstitch the bottom of the sleeve to the backing.

Binding

Refer to the projects for recommended strip widths.

1. Measure the outside edges of your quilt; add 6". Cut fabric strips to this measurement.
2. With right sides together, place one strip across the other at right angles as shown. Stitch a 45°-angle seam. Trim excess fabric and press seams open.

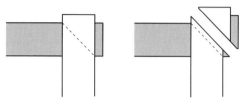

3. Fold the strip in half lengthwise, wrong sides together, and press. Cut one end of the strip at a 45° angle and turn under ¼". This is the beginning of your binding.

Making Pegs for Hanging Quilts

1. Purchase two ¾"-diameter dowels. Cut 1 dowel into 3"-long segments. Make *every other cut* at a 45° angle.

2. Drill a 1"-deep hole, the diameter of the nail, in the center of the side cut at a 45° angle. I recommend 2" finishing nails.

3. Put a little glue in the hole. Place a 2" finishing nail in the hole.
4. Stain if desired. Attach dowel pegs to the wall at a 45° angle.
5. Measure the quilt and cut the remaining dowel 4" longer than the width of the quilt. Hang the quilt on the pegs.

4. Starting on one side of the quilt, just to the right of the center, sew the binding to the quilt. Use a ¼"-wide seam allowance. Keep the raw edges of the binding even with the quilt-top edge. End the stitching ¼" from the corner of the quilt and backstitch.

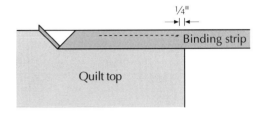

TIP

Hold the binding even with the quilt edge, rather than pinning, so you can smooth it into place as you stitch.

5. Lift the presser foot and move the needle to the up position. Turn the quilt so you will be stitching down the next side. Fold the fabric up, away from the quilt.

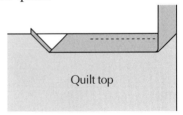

6. Fold the binding down, parallel with the edge of the quilt top. Start stitching ¼" from the edge. Repeat for remaining corners.

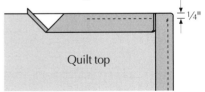

7. When you reach the beginning, overlap the stitches about 1" and trim the excess binding at a 45° angle. Tuck the end of the binding into the fold and finish the seam.

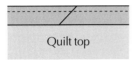

8. Fold the binding to the back, covering stitching. Blindstitch. Tuck the corners to form miters.

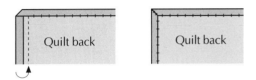

SIGNING YOUR QUILT

Like any artwork, a quilt isn't finished until it is signed and dated. The projects in this book offer some fun ways to sign your quilt. You should include the name of the quilt, where it was made, who made it, when it was made, and the recipient, relationship, and occasion if it was made as a gift. You might even want to add care instructions. Future generations will thank you for remembering to sign your quilt.

RECORDING YOUR QUILTMAKING

Keep a record or journal of your quilts. Take a picture of your completed quilt. Glue the picture onto a sheet of paper. Record all pertinent information about the quilt on the page, and place it in a plastic sheet protector. Save these pages in a notebook.

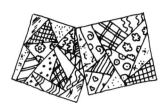

About the Author

Hollie Milne is a gifted quilt designer and creator. She has been piecing quilt tops, quilting by hand and machine, and teaching the art of quiltmaking for more than twenty years.

Hollie's quilting developed around her family. For her first baby, she cross-stitched and hand quilted a delightful coverlet. For her second baby, she pieced her first quilt (this was before the rotary cutter). After her third baby, Hollie began giving quilts she had made to family and friends. She began to teach quiltmaking after her fourth baby, and after her fifth and last baby, Hollie turned her focus to designing quilts and machine quilting.

Today, Hollie's life is filled with quilting, and her family proudly supports her dedication to this art. She says, "In the midst of piecing a quilt top, I became aware of the special vitality that quilting has brought to my days and the meaning it has added to my life. As my family grew, so did my love of quilting."

Hollie has made more than one hundred quilts. Her creations adorn her walls, beds, and cupboards. Indeed, her home is a celebration of the art of quiltmaking.